Lilies & Lace
&
Dark Pretty
Things

Poetry from the Heart

Other Books by Melody Lee

Moon Gypsy
Vine: Book of Poetry
Season of the Sorceress

Lilies & Lace & Dark Pretty Things

Poetry from the Heart

Melody Lee

Lilies & Lace & Dark Pretty Things

ISBN: 978-1-7341931-0-7

Library of Congress Control Number: 2019919257

Editor: Ashley Jane
Cover and Illustrations: Angie Shea

Books may be purchased in bulk for promotional, educational, or business use.

First Edition: January 2020

Introduction & Dedication

Dreams are the seeds of flowers.
They must be nurtured
to grow, bloom, and thrive.
Dreams are caterpillars
waiting to turn into butterflies.
They are baby birds learning to fly.
Poetry in motion, thoughts coming to life.

If you are a returning reader, thank you. It delights me that you have returned for more of my ever-growing garden of poetry. If you are a new reader, welcome, and thank you for being here. I hope you enjoy the world you are about to enter. My words are dedicated to the dreamers, the free-spirited, the romantics and the rebels, the lovers and the healers, and to each of you, my readers.

Table of Contents

Watercolors

&

Pomegranates

Undress my soul one petal at a time.

Holy Water

Sometimes the moon is my muse,
like at 2 a.m. when I am wide awake
confessing my sins,
secrets,
desires
to something 238,855 miles away,
yet right outside my window
listening to the strum of my heartbeat.

Sometimes nature is my muse,
pouring her majestic sky into my soul,
filling me with divine inspiration.

Then there is you,
like holy water
falling on my rosy skin,
cleansing me
of past transgressions,
seeing beyond
the physical, the flaws,
accepting all of me.

When we kiss there is only you and me.
I forget the world and its rotations,

the moon and its shadows,
and colors,
and eclipses.
There's only the sun and the stars.

You are my obscure poetry.
My night and my day.
My favorite muse.

Loud and Hard

I don't know how to love or feel
in soft pale colors.
I love loud and hard
and, ultimately, I hurt the same way.

May Is the Color of Pomegranates

When May arrives and the afternoon sky
bursts with pink fire and ripe tangerines
you will reminisce how she was
volcanic passion
swirling like a tornado in the middle
of a rainstorm

her eyes wild with life
her hair wavy
and scarlet red

remember how she danced
her dress sticking to her body
like honey to its hive

every playful curve intoxicating you
her nipples
were torpedoes and all you wanted to do
was crawl under her alabaster skin
and drink in her heat

she'd open her mouth
swallowing the rain

she was like the storm itself
a fox, a wolf, an animal unleashed
always a little psychotic
when it came to love
over the edge hardly described her

but she knew how to live, *did she ever*
and she knew how to love
all consuming
never half-in
she'd make you the brightest star
in her galaxy
she'd bloody kill you
if you betrayed her heart
you'd never be the same again
after loving her

May is the month of blossoming gardens
and savage skies, thunderstorms
and curiosity

May is the month of falling and blooming
and rising in love

Wildfires

Beware of sunsets beaming
in lovers' eyes: golden, alluring,
dramatic, hypnotic.
They become wildfires without notice.

The Taste of Love

You kissed me
Delicate and fierce
I heard the song of nightingales
Inspiring love
And the moon was on fire
You kissed me
All the stars
Touched my hair
And there was lightning everywhere
You kissed me
Sweet sensation
Causing butterfly dips
Heart palpitations
I heard the wolf in your throat
And tasted love on your tongue
A contradiction too pure to ignore
I kissed you back
Desperate for more
My probing tongue reaching your heart
This is the making of a beautiful love affair

Erotic Love Story

We had deep, soul penetrating conversation
with our eyes; it was magical,
it was dangerous,
and it was the most erotic love story
I had heard in a long, long while.

Sundress

I bought a pretty little sundress
sweet and sexy
at a charming shop
today
near the beach
yellow like the sun
with magenta and teal leaf designs
to lift my mood

Brings out the fire in my wavy hair
florals and flowers and the sea
and thoughts of you and me

You always loved it
when I wore sundresses
I'll wear mine in remembrance of you

Sharing rum runners
and wine slushies on hot summer days
barefoot in the warm sand
getting toasty and tanned

indulging in the
best
  ever
    kisses

Memories of you and me
forever. Isn't that how it
was supposed to be?

Once in a Lifetime

They both suffer in silence. It was real,
it was true, but some things can't be fixed,
and that is a damn shame for those loves
that were so powerful, those souls that
were so connected. There will never be
another love quite the same, or even half
as intense for either of them. So, they
continue living, tortured, without each
other.

The Diary

I plucked the petals
off the pink lilies and peonies
you gave me and placed them
between the pages of Anais Nin's Diary,
Volume One.

I moved away,
packed my books,
life happened,
and I forgot.

Years later I opened the diary—
Petals fell out scattering
beneath my heart,
on the floor beside my bare feet.

Suddenly, the love we shared
all those years
and tears ago blossomed
underneath my aching bosom.
Memories stuck in time
began flooding my eyes,
dripping down my cheeks,
reviving poems etched in my bones
from long ago.

Those dead flowers
bled life that day,
resurrecting your name
on my tongue,
pumping you back
into my bloodstream
like the drug you always were,
returning our love
to the poetry it always was.

Immortal Souls

People will always come and go
in your life,
but the souls of those
meant to stay,
even if only in your heart,
will never disappear.

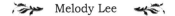

Someone Who Understood

She never needed a deep *thinker*, she
needed a deep *feeler*, someone who
understood, and maybe that's the same
thing.

Tangled

I'm a tangled mess
of wild
and I don't want to be
unraveled.
I like me this way.

Promised Land

It's not loneliness that frightens me
It's the way you feel like the morning sun
and tenderness
It's the way I need to swim into you
A warm ocean covering wounded skin
A soft blanket of buttery light
It's the way I enjoy your vibe, the soft
Comfort I feel with you
Harmonic waves in sync
with my energy
Yin and Yang
It's the way you subtly destroy
My safe zone
Nimbly I collapse into you
More than I care to admit
A baby bird falling
from its nest, you sweep me up
Saving me
Unmoved by my crimes
Undeterred by random moods
You feel like a dream to which
I could get accustomed
You feel like rebirth
A savior rescuing souls

I'm orbiting around Jupiter
Seeing the spheres of Saturn
Getting closer to the sun
Forgetting my fears
Bringing me to the promised land
Medicine man
Healing kiss to my heart
Letting go
Uninhibited
I am unafraid

Little Death

I've tasted your mind
and inhaled your essence,
but the way we become one...
Oh, the way our bodies
merge as we dance into each
other, is a little death I want
again
and again.

Saltwater

Too much seawater consumed by humans
dehydrates and destroys brains cells,
causing delirium, before succumbing
to death.

The ocean, quite the mystery—
Deceptively gentle and peaceful.

A ferocious beast, the ocean could
swallow one whole; yet it is calm and serene.
It is deep and dark and wild and dangerous,
and we love it, worship it. We travel to it,
swim in it, vacation near it, take cruises on
it, study it, write about it. The seas can
destroy as quickly as they can heal. We
adore the ocean for all its paradoxes. Always
have. Always will.

My god, how the ocean is intensely arousing
and intriguing and all at once consuming.
Strange attraction. Eternal enigma.

Sometimes love is like the ocean.
                Sometimes love is the sea.

Deepest

Beauty is skin deep,
but I crave something deeper.
I want to drown in the depths
of your soul.

Lilies & Lace
& Dark Pretty Things

There are days I am scared
to open up and let the world
see the beautiful tragedy
breathing in me. I am not
all soft petals and pretty lace.

Cynthia and You

Sunsets.
Muscle beach and fast cars.
Remembering that summer
I snuck away, flying
out west on a big airplane.
Addicted to all the wrong things,
but really, they weren't.
I needed art to write poetry.
I needed muses to create poems.
I needed experiences to have stories.
I needed you to realize
I didn't need you.
I needed me to realize that, too.

We went for German beer
at your favorite pub,
bought gourmet coffee
for our late mornings.
As we perused trendy shops
along Newport Beach,
skateboarders zoomed past us.
Seagulls overhead.

Suddenly, I am reminded
of Jonathon Livingston, by Richard Bach;

how that lone seagull needed to be lost
to find himself.
To understand his purpose on Earth.
To learn to fly. You are talking to me
and I only hear your voice,
not your words.
I'm daydreaming of Jonathon
learning to fly.

An afternoon walking
amongst the lush gardens
at the J. Paul Getty Museum.
I enjoyed that trip with you.
I would return. I would savor more
of the flowers and the sky.
I would remember to take more pictures
and buy less art books.
An evening attending a party of some
of your LA music friends.
The irony: No one played their instruments
or sang their songs. No dancing.
No food. Only Cheetos
and potato chips, does that count?
This is what you called a party.
I was bored, just thought you should know.

Walking on Santa Monica Pier,

just me this time,
toes in the sand,
ankles in the cold Pacific sea.

Later, after English tea
and my first ever scone,
cranberry and orange,
I watched Bridget Jones Diary
alone
in a Santa Monica theater.
I was dreaming of him being there.
Holding my hand,
maybe even watching me.

But really, without even realizing it
at the time, I was falling in love with me.
My wings were new, unexercised.
I needed you to realize
I didn't need you.
I needed me to realize that, too.

These are the little big things I recount
as I mentally revisit that summer I
went to see you. To see him. To see LA.
To find me.

Broken Rainbows

Break a writer's heart and watch her
become an explosion of creativity.
That's what happens
with all the shattered pieces
of a lovelorn heart; like magic,
they turn into mosaics of art.

Poets turn blood into roses
            and tears into sunsets.

Red Berries

I've moaned into the crevices
of your mind, you've bloomed
in the landscape of mine. I've
turned our days into luscious red berries
and lived on them frugally. They enrich
my wine, and I savor each sweet sip
as if it might be my last.

Our souls have touched a thousand times
in a thousand different ways. Loving you
all these years has opened another
dimension of love.

But I am greedy, the primal sense
of touch, skin on skin,
clings like jasmine to my veins.
I need more, I am ready. It's time.

A craving built from more
than the chemistry of words
slowly becoming mute, lost
as the years wash away.
Don't
Don't
Don't let that happen.

I want to open for you like pink azaleas
in the morning sun. Our bodies
beautifully fitted, the joining of rivers.

Take my hand, don't be afraid.
I will nurture your dominance
and my submission will be
at your command
as we breathe life into the mystery.

I'm tired of only words.
Don't
Don't
Don't make me wait any longer, a door
I've opened
only to find the door locked all along.

Perfect Sin

Last night
a full moon
You were there
I was here but I
could still feel your heartbeat
and your fingers
digging into my skin
as your famished mouth
took me all in
Could you hear my howl
under the violet sky?
Feel our perfect sin?
When the trees rustled
and the ground shook
could you sense me there?
Could you hear me
whispering your name
in the wind?

Beast

She's an angel waiting
for her beast to come
tear off her wings, leave bite
marks between her thighs,
and scarlet kisses on her heart.

All or Nothing

Kiss me in poetry
or don't kiss me at all.
Love me down
to my bare bones,
my skin and my soul
or not at all.

Poetry, one simply can't get
more naked than that.

Resilience

Hearts ripped into thousands of pieces,
yet we pick up all the broken parts,
wash the blood, the stains, the ashes
down the drain, and tuck that love
behind our ribs, moving forward
with breathtaking grace, resolve
and strength.
We still believe in the power of love.
We know real love exists, even
after years of deception.
We are wiser. We are resilient.

The heartbroken are the strongest,
most beautiful of souls; they have
opened their hearts fully to love,
been deceived by love.
They have cried alone
and cleaned up the mess alone.
The broken hearted have loved selflessly,
putting another first. And yet, they still
love with the purest of hearts,

and this is hauntingly,
beautifully breathtaking.

Written for all the strong, courageous, and
heartbroken women and men who press forward
despite their crushed hearts, who still have hope
and believe in the power of love.

Lemon Pies

A house filled with beauty
rotting from the death of love

Fruit flies congregate
around overripe bananas
and the birdbath is dry

Television blares
drowning out
screaming silences

Subliminal messages
darting like noisy ghosts in the room
Onlookers don't understand

Life is not as it seems
but the squirrels keep visiting
and the artist keeps creating

She's cleaning the closets
and making lemon pies

The Crow from Long Ago

Minding my own affairs
dreaming of god knows what
those many years ago
under a seemingly calm
South Florida sun
happy times
when the boys were young
cherished memories

Out of nowhere, a crow swooping
from a skeletal palm tree
attacks my head, not a care
in the world that earlier I had it styled
and paid pretty bucks
to get my hair just so

The grumpy old black bird, or perhaps
young nervous momma bird, wants a nip
of my skull
underneath my long tresses
a peck
a warning
pay attention you've come too close
I've got babies, you're on my turf

Never again did I venture
too close, yet that anorexic tree
couldn't be entirely avoided
during my mid-morning walks

Besides, my curiosity
always got the best of me

As I approached, I'd pick up my pace
swerving around
steering clear
of any possible surprise attacks
Forevermore careful not to intrude
where I'm not wanted
But still curious...

Field of Green

Remembering that day last Spring
you called me on the phone
and I met you in a hazy dream
You read me Thoreau's *Walden*
on an open field of green
chanting *"All good things*
are wild and free."
I wrote poetry
on the inside of your mouth
Juicy and pink
A delicious memory
Indelible ink
Heated, we stripped our clothes
and bared our souls. Took a dip
in a cool running stream
splashing, until we became two soft waves
merging as one body of water
You made me scream, oh
how you made me scream
Wild daisies grew between my toes
Rosebuds under my clothes
I still hide our flesh-covered poems
in the red corner of my heart.

Seven Continents

Never realized how much I could
love one man.
Didn't know I could possibly love him
more than I already do...until he said
he was addicted to me.
My heart must be the size
of seven continents by now.

Tonight

Tonight, all the cells in my body
are missing you. Not just my mind
or my body or my thoughts, but
every damn cell
down to the nucleus
of my soul, to the fabric of my being.

Heartbeat

Out of sight
out of mind
as they say,
but the heart
is a different beat
all together.

...Damn Heart

Rapture

You stood by the ocean's edge
wearing nothing but moonlight.
Your hair blowing in the wind,
purple waves
crashing at your feet.
I coveted the onyx sky

enveloping your heavenly skin.
The raging sea, enchanted by sorcery
in your eyes, became calm. You
were like the rapture

inhabiting the atmosphere,
coming for me, building a home
in my brokenness. Making me whole.
I felt alive for the first time
in a long time.
And your eyes, crystalline

and omnipotent, felt my stare,
captivated,
from behind the dunes.

You, a mysterious figure in the night.

I the onlooker,
mesmerized. Three flashes of lightning

and the earth moved. I was
falling deeply under your spell.
You turned your head
suddenly
slowly

looked straight at me,
engulfing my heart, piercing
my soul. I saw infinity
drape my feet.
I felt the sky gift me light.

Final Kiss

I have a stack of regrets.
They've bogged me down for years,
but today,
today I drove to the ocean
and brought my heavy bag along.
Today I tossed all those regrets
to the sea,
released them to the sky,
with nothing more
than a final kiss goodbye.

Learning Curve

Mistakes are simply learning opportunities.
Sadness serves a purpose,
especially for poets
and writers and artsy types.
And all those regrets,
well, it's silly to regret
what once made you happy.

My dual conversations, internal opposing views.
I play devil's advocate with myself.

Soul Meets Soul
in the Floating Twilight

We made love fully clothed
Piercing each other's minds
with tender sultry caresses
and throbbing thrusts, soul
against soul
Spiritual and ethereal
A feeling of floating in twilight
with the shimmering stars
and learning all their names
A luscious kind of love, the best
kind of love, perfection
and sometimes this is all we need

Milk and Honey

Grey clouds splatter
blood of despair,
rain becomes red.

Pity parties, self-loathing, bitterness
like poison herbs. A curse.
You turn the dagger inward
slashing your own heart, jumping
off your own bridge. Your lungs
deflate. Tearing yourself apart
with your many crowns of thorns.
Nothing good crystalizes from habitual
self-hate.

Harvest instead milk and honey.
Let the turnips and garlic rot.
Remove the self-inflicted dagger.
Remove the curse. Lick the wounds
and place the jewels back on your head.
Look how beautifully you clean up—
Inside and out you beam like a sunflower,
illuminating like a bright star in a charcoal
sky.

Geese

A family of geese strolls
across the two-lane road.
In no hurry, they waddle a straight line
in their geese-like way.
People have places to go,
deadlines to meet.
I brake and let them pass.
The other cars brake, too.
At this moment, these geese
reaching their destination
are more important than any of us
behind our wheels reaching our
destinations,

and this is when I know the heart of man
is inherently good and kind.

For all the ugly, bad, evil in the world,
a group of drivers stopped, giving these
migrating, aquatic birds the right-of-way.
A smile forms inside my heart.
I am pleased.
Today will be a good day.
Silly flock of geese,
you saved the day in your goose-like way.

The Blink of an Eye

June lands on the windowpane
All too soon
A blue butterfly
One final cool breeze
Summer around the bend
I haven't packed away Spring
Slow it down
The snow of winter falls on my knees
At the blink of an eye, it leaves

The Lumineers stuck in my head
Ophelia, catchy song
Dancing barefoot in the grass
With the insects and the ants
Tasting the music
like it's essential for life

Feeling the earth as if it's
Attached to my soul
Toes digging in the ground
Prolonging the moment
Making it last

The month will come and go

As will the season
In a flash
Savor every moment
Kiss with your eyes closed
Love with your heart fully open
Take it slow
All of it
Life
Love
Everything

Guiding Light

Writing poetry is like
        putting a knife
               into your soul
                      and slicing
                             slicing
                                     slicing

        and yet,
               poetry
                      is my guiding light

Blooming Roses

&

Black Holes

Maybe I had thorns on my tongue—
words I said,
the way I spoke, but my heart was always
growing roses.

Suddenly

I love how the air
changes—
You can feel it.
You can smell it.
And suddenly it is autumn,
and my heart is full of life.

Renewal

I'm returning to the mountains.
I'll kiss the trees and touch the stars.
I'll bring the moon to my heart
and leave my handprint in the sky.

I'm returning to the mountains.
I'll fall again, the way lovers do,
in full open ecstasy, this time unscathed.

I'm returning to the mountains,
a retreat with myself, a rest
from the rat-race.

I'm returning to the mountains
to mediate and renew.

Flowerbeds

You'll find her blossoming
around midnight,
growing flowerbeds
under the satellite.
She's a stay-up-late, weird,
talk to the moon, dance
under constellations girl.

Time & Space

There's a space
between dark and light,
and it's where you and I exist.

Galaxies collide.
Comets shatter.
Time doesn't matter
when we kiss.

Magnetism

Pay attention to the way souls meet
and the energy between them.
It's not called magnetism for nothing.
Souls recognize each other.

Reflection

You are a mirrored reflection
of your thoughts. Keep them high.
Keep them mighty. Let your
manifestation be ten thousand rays of light.

Dark energies will never consume you
        because you are abundant starlight.

Character

Entice me with your mind,
not your material possessions
or fancy things.
Show me your heart, not your biceps
and six pack pecs.
Don't get me wrong, I like nice things
and fit, sculpted bodies, but I prefer
a deep soul, kind heart, and strong mind.
If you want to keep me interested,
it will need to be something
deeper than the shallow end.

For my boys—
If you want to keep her interested,
show her the deeper things in your life.
Show her your soul.

Temporal Things

I used to surround myself with noise
and people and things. I thought
that's what I needed to be happy,
to be content, to fill an ever-growing void,
but those temporal things made me
restless, always wanting more,
craving something out of reach.

As I've gotten older, I have found that
my own company, good music, and books
are perfectly sufficient and often
more fulfilling.

Trust

We guard ourselves—
To the world, we seem cold and hard.
The truth is we love the hardest.
We have huge, giving,
compassionate hearts,
ready to pour out love
when we feel safe and secure.

And I'm Reminded

You keep me at arm's length
when I yearn to be closer,
your shoulder.
To be near your cheek, your face,
your mouth,
your tongue.
When I want to look into your eyes,
you don't allow me
to look deeply into them.
When I need to be next to your heart,
to hear it beat while next to mine,
you outstretch your arm
inviting me to prop on it, only
for a while.
Not too close.

And I'm reminded, I'm like a butterfly,
fierce
and fragile and free.
So, I'll remain your bird in flight
as your arm
outstretches for me to temporarily
perch, never to stay.
You made it this way, and I am reminded
...*I'll never be yours.*

70

Ghosts

I believe in love; its ghosts forever
haunt me. Its shadow follows me
into the darkness. It's everywhere I go
and in everything I do. Love's presence
lingers in the atmosphere.
A grip like the clamping of teeth on skin.

Resonate

I understood the ominous sky
because it was so much like you,
and I was a blazing, bleeding sun
always willing to burn
for our love.

Soul Pain

When the heart
and the head
are at constant odds
with each other,
it can be a real pain
in the soul.

Pay Attention

The universe always
has our best interest,
if only we would be still,
quiet our minds and pay attention.

True Beauty

Beauty comes from struggles, from falling over and over and getting up again and again. It comes from roadblocks, figuring a way around them and working through them. It comes from being braver than your fears. From heartbreak and hundreds of tears. True beauty is all the battles you have conquered. Perseverance, patience, determination, grit. And, of course, the beauty of being a genuinely compassionate human surpasses everything. There is nothing more truly gorgeous than a kind soul, which makes one's entire aura radiate.

If you wish to be beautiful
      search your heart, for it is
            there where love emanates
                and beauty radiates.

Both

It's beautiful when you
can be both soft and fire
angel and vixen.

To survive in this, sometimes, cruel world
one needs a fierce mix of both.

Thunder

If you don't like storms
and aren't prepared for hurricanes,
better stay away from her calm seas,
for lightning courses through her
blue-fire veins and underneath
that soft exterior roars thunder.

Water

I am **water**, but don't be deceived into thinking I am weak, for then you will not be on guard when I drown you in my depth or burn out your fire. Both my boiling and freezing temperatures are capable of destroying. Yet I am love and empathy, destruction is not my desire. My element has empowered me with intuition, both a blessing and a curse. Like a river nymph, a goddess of the sea, a mermaid queen, I am an eternal mystery. Calm, serene, wickedly wild. Loving almost to the point of madness, I will silently consume you. Water, the most craved and feared element; if left without, one becomes desperate for it. If venturing too far into its depths, one is devoured by it.

Water, My Element

Moonflower

She's a moonflower blooming
between the lonely parts
of your ribcage. She'll begin
with a slow dance around your spine,
until, unexpectedly, you feel her
twirling in the forefront of your mind.
Soon, she'll be blossoming violets
in the ocean of your heart,
lighting up your darkest nights.
Like Cassiopeia in the northern sky,
her beauty unrivaled, dazzling and timeless.

Red Riding Hood

Sweet little Red Riding Hood
was secretly a savage little sorceress
who ran around casting spells on *beasts*,
cursing them with feral love
and famished kisses,
hellfire, and holy water.

Fight

You need a love that stirs
your soul and exhilarates
all five senses, physical
and spiritual, and sometimes
that means the occasional hair
pulling and punching in the gut.
Not in the literal sense, rather, to
wake you up and realize there is
something worth fighting for.

Captured

My mind traces the edges of his.
I hear him,
even when he doesn't say a word.
I feel his soul,
aware of his fears, his sadness,
his darkest desires.
My fingertips feel his sins.
My tongue, my mouth, my lips
know all his secrets.
He is brave and bold
and fierce like a mountain lion,
and I am stronger for loving this savage
gentleman.

We are two beasts
caught in the heart's trap
of each other.
In tune with his energy, my movements
unconsciously synchronize with his,
and his with mine,
yet I am my own rhythm,
and he is his own beat.
It's a little a bit of sorcery
and a whole lot of magical love.

Call it what you will,
but the heart knows love
when it bleeds it.
The heart knows a powerful connection
when it's seized by it.
The heart can't sing sweetly
when it's left desolate, without this
extraordinary love.

The Cracks of My Ribs

Your love grew between the cracks
of my ribs like ivy clinging to a tree,
eager to reach the light. On the contrary,
your love didn't suffocate me, nor did it
hoard my energy; it took root in my soul
providing sweet nectar to my heart,
and I burst like a magical sunbeam
when you reached my peak.

Your hands and fingers
foraging every curve, every part
of my soft flesh, piercing my soul
with the dark flame
of your eyes.
My lips famished for the taste
of your salty skin,
You are my beautiful savage.

I'm not suffocating.
I'm new syncopated life.
I am yours.
The tree to your vine.
The air in your lungs. I am nothing
without you
and everything with you.

You are mine. Stronger and divine
with my love,
my holy master.

You have grown wildly between the cracks
of my ribs
embedding your beauty like a tattoo
into my bones.
Molten lava flowing into my bloodstream.
And I am more beauty for giving you
my whole heart.

Pulse

If poetry is madness, I choose madness.
If love is insanity, I choose insanity.
There is nothing worse in life
than numbness,
than feeling dead while having a pulse.

My Greatest Love

You were the blackbird
resting on my shoulder,
making a home in the sweetest
rosebud of my heart.

Soul Flame

Even on your worst days, he'll
pull you close and hold you tight.
He won't give up on you. He'll stay
and fight. He's your counterpart,
your soul flame.

Losing My Faith

Those poems
Those vapid poems dressed up
in skimpy lingerie and stilettos
Light like pale flowers
Falling petals
All smoky and pretty
but pallid as starving girls
Unimaginative
Diaphanous
Lacking substance
  a breaking branch
  flimsy foundation
  overused themes
making me lose my faith
in the art of inspiring ink
I want a book of poems that when I
finish reading, I exclaim, "Damn,
I wish I wrote like that!"

Just to be Clear

I am inspired by many,
but am in competition
with only myself.

Blooming Roses in June

I kissed a girl one electrifying afternoon,
took her luscious mouth
and loved her up and down.
She tasted like sunshine and
felt like blooming roses in June.
Some assertive force of nature
—chemistry can be hypnotic like that—
compelled this bashful girl
to pull her close,
cherishing her sweet forbidden lips,
adoring them with my mouth,
my teeth, my tongue. She eagerly
returned the love right back to me. We
felt comfortable, like home, like we were
meant to be.

It was diamonds falling from the sky
kind of magic—delicious, delirious,
decadent.
I'd do it all again.

This poem was written as a word prompt
Challenge for #PrideAnthemThemeWord
Phrase: I kissed a girl

Wild

Wild shows up
in her messy hair,
her sassy grin,
the glimmer in her curious eyes.

And only the perceptive will notice.

I Do - The Paradox of Us

I do not trust your tongue,
though I admit, it cast a spell on me.
You have enchanted me.

I do not trust your words,
though I confess, they
make me feel cherished and pretty.
I like the way we blend, together.

I do not trust your tongue—
your kind of charming is dangerous,
though I like the way you hear me;
you listen when I speak, when I tell you
my dreams, where I've been,
places I want to go, people I've met,
music I love, movies I've seen,
my favorite meals, what I like to wear,
and who I want to be when I "grow up."
I like reading you poetry
and the way you encourage me to write
more.

I do not trust the sugar
falling sweet from your lips.

I see right through
the seductive disguise,
though I admit that witty, clever tongue
challenges me, and I respect a healthy
challenge.
You are brilliant.

I do not trust your mouth,
your lips,
your tongue,
when they touch mine.
Magnetism pulling me down
like an undercurrent
I've not the will to fight.

But I do trust the chemistry
between us. The magic of us.
I do trust the interlocking
of our hearts
as our minds ignite
and our tongues collide
and our bodies burn.
Bringing me to the edge,
you make me squirm.

I do trust your tongue when I
feel its energy

dutifully trying to be better,
making demands on me,
lifting me to the sky,
through the clouds,
touching sunbeams.
You intrigue me.

I do trust your tongue,
the way it guides and feels
and tastes like vanilla and caramel
and forbidden apples—
the perfect paradox of you
...of us.

Dinner with Poe

I like dirty fairytales.
I like them even better
when you read them to me.

Making Art

Handcuff me in poetry
Your tongue is the pen
Your love is the ink
Let me be your canvas
Turn me into A R T

The Trap of the Black Cat

I warned him about the river running
through my soul, the black cat living
inside me. I warned him of the rush
of just one kiss, like a spell,
he wouldn't have the will to leave.
But it was too late, he tasted my flame,
lapped it up like hot holy nectar,
and unearthed divinity hidden
like a forbidden secret beneath my skin.

High

I got high on her magic,
drunk on her emerald cat eyes.
She's a clever a little one,
dazzling witch in disguise.

Possess

I won't beg for your love
but I will
gently hold your lovely face
behind shadows under a starry night
tracing the soft edges with my fingertips
feel you squirm
while gazing deep into your eyes
until you're in a trance like state
ah, yes, hypnotized
then I'll kiss those luscious ruby lips
bite down on the purity of your long
exquisite neck
until you blush like red cherry pie
mark you
and make you mine
...forever.

A Great Love Affair

Spending hours in libraries
and used bookstores. Skipping meals.
Losing track of time, she has done this.
She is stubborn like that. It's because
of her great love affair with words
and books, two things in her life
that are constant.

There's something charming
        and quite sexy about used bookstores.

Falling in Connection

I want to delve
into your mind,
explore its twists
and turns, rub
against your soul
and get locked
inside your heart.

Oxygen

She loves making out
in the poetry section of libraries.
The smell of old books turns her on,
and if you read to her
from the classics, her senses heighten.

She kisses me as if I am oxygen,
right there, between Neruda and
Dickinson.
She is the drug, and I, the addict.
Smelling of lilacs,
gardenias and dusty books,
her lips are as alluring as Tupelo honey.

I need her—her voluminous mind,
her taste, her love; all of her—
like the writer needs paper & ink,
like the bibliophile needs books,

and she needs me like the book
needs the reader. Without each other
we barely breathe, hardly function—
Darkness invades, suffocation sets in.

She's the dark nerdy forest.
I am the sapiosexual predator.
She's poetry, and I, her ultimate muse.

Wait

The right one will fall in love
with the taste of your kind of demons.
Don't settle for anything less.

Poetry and Rationality

Poetry is a lot like love;
it's not always rational,
that's not its intention.
If you want rational,
read a scientific journal
or a chemistry book.

Requirement

If you are not a lover of literature,
poetry, books, and you don't relate
to my love of them, my need for them,
then I can't fall in love with you,
and don't call us soulmates.

Tribe

I never needed a large clan
surrounding me.
I feared the worm,
the rotten apple,
the suffocation.
I always felt lighter,
freer,
happier,
with a few loyal friends
I could safely call
my tribe.

Clouds

Got to love a little Plath
mixed with Edgar Allan Poe
on a dark, gloomy day.
Menacing clouds levitate
around my heart,
and the raven wants to play.

Dinner with Poe

I light candles, unscented,
and listen to the hauntingly
poignant music of Beach House

Read Sylvia Plath
and Edgar Allan Poe,
Ariel and *Annabel Lee,*
alone in my one-room apartment
smelling of fresh paint and used books
on a gray, gloomy afternoon
in the middle of spring

Dreaming of the sea
Dreaming of a love
the way Poe loved Annabel Lee

Sliding into melancholy
I am slipping away
candles burning
mind stirring
preparing for the dance
Clouds become heavy and ashy
like cold charcoal

Looming Norway maples

outside my window
somber in the dead of spring
in sync with my mood as I read
and dream
think and scheme

They sway, the maples
sway like immortal lovers
waiting for their true loves to return
from war

A squirrel clutching his acorn treasure
eyes darting
always on alert
ready to flee
occupied
feeding his little belly
nourishing his little self
entertaining me and Plath and Poe
in his little feisty nonchalant way
underneath the swaying maple trees

I read and imagine
romancing words
weeping like the willows growing
near the lake where I go to pray

On my playlist, Lana Del Rey
laments about hope
being a dangerous thing
for a woman like her
like me

And there I am with Poe reminiscing
about his one true love, Annabel Lee
The suicide spirit of Plath
keeping me company
in the eclipse of my mind

Those maples, bending and dancing
mystically ethereal, enchant me
A squirrel oblivious to my presence
Music freeing me in its melancholic melody

There's something about losing yourself
in music and the words of dead poets, only
to find the most truth you've ever known.

Jaguar

Obsessed with the dark spheres
in his eyes; the way they search,
finding the moon's shadow in mine,
the way they awaken the primal in me,
conjuring fire in parts I didn't know
existed, between my ribs,
between my toes, my scalp, my belly,
my lungs, my cheeks, my nose.

Obsessed with the way he
destroys me in all the right ways.
I crave that destruction
when we are apart.
I am falling helplessly.
His scent, his smile…
that mischievous grin.
His sleek movements
lure me
and I ache for his touch.

He's the beast knocking on my heart,
breathing in my lungs
full of dreams and dangerous magic.

114

We Loved

He loved me to the point
of madness,
and I could not have asked
for anything greater.

Ache

There is an ache behind my throat
and a longing in my lungs
when we depart.
You are my breath
and the ground
holding me to the earth.

Trying

I'm trying to let go,
but he ravished my soul
and took residence in my heart.
Not so easy to discard
a connection like that,
even if it is with a beast
of a man.

Hell

Now I know what hell is—
It's my soul desperately
trying to detach from yours.
My ears not hearing your voice.
My lips not touching yours.
My heart trying to stop yearning.
Unsuccessfully.

Hell is you not here with me.

As If

He told me I better not write about him
in my poetry, as if my heartbreak
could remain silent,
as if my comeback had a choice.

When my heart is overcome with grief,
it bleeds, and that involves a bit of
screaming.

The Difference

Sometimes they lash out
because they are hurting,
and sometimes they lash out
because they are monsters.
Understand the difference.

Detoxification

Currently in the middle
of crucifying bad attitudes,
negativity, and poisonous relationships.
Clearing my chakras and finding my peace.

Finished

There's no room for two here
with us, so decide what you want
before you come knocking back
on my heart. I am finished
with cowards, and I'm done
settling for less than what I deserve.

Make up your mind, or I'll make it up for you.

Time

Time doesn't completely
diminish the flame
in my heart,
but it doesn't burn for you
the way it once did.

Karma

Darling, I forgave you long ago.
It's karma that never forgets
and always bites.

Actions

If you constantly
question their actions,
or lack of,
it's not an issue with you,
it's an issue with them.

Let's Be Clear

Some people confuse my sweet nature and gentle heart for weakness. Let's be clear, once I detect bullshit, sweet and gentle is not what you'll get from me. Let's be clear, if I've been kind to you, supportive, loyal and you betray my friendship, tenderness from me is not what you'll see. Let's be clear about this, I am not weak. I am kind. Huge difference. I am not weak. I just have a heart full of love. And, oh, what strength there is in filling the world with love.

Fill the world with love.

Free Your Soul

Forgiveness is a beautiful thing—for you,
not necessarily for them. It releases you
from the dark grip of anger, regret,
and other toxic emotions. It clears your
path for new and good energy. It frees your
soul.

In a World of Butterflies

She was a raven in a world
of butterflies.
A purple orchid in a field
of bright flowers.
Never quite fitting in, but
damn if she didn't have the
sweetest ever mischievous
grin. One couldn't help but
be captivated by the aura
that was everywhere she went.

Lines & Boxes

Straight lines
frighten me.
I've never been good
at narrow thinking
or perfect order.

I'm not a box kind of gal, so stop
                    trying to make me fit in one.

Secrets

Don't tell your secrets to anyone
who doesn't see the beauty in weird,
who is uncomfortable out of the box,
bending, or taking a different route,
and, most importantly, who doesn't
believe in magic.

The Light

She faced her demons
and the darkness
and finally understood
how they led her to the light.

Learn to find the light
        within your own darkness.
                It's there. I promise.

My Unicorn

You can't be magical if you're too busy
being cynical. So, get off your high horse
and come join me on my unicorn.

I will always be the crazy one
            who believes in magic, mermaids,
                        and impossible dreams.

Melody Lee

Acknowledgements

Ashley Jane. Thank you for reading my manuscript and your assistance with my book and cover layout, for your extra time, and most importantly, for your friendship.
Angie Shea Waters. Thank you for approaching me with your beautiful palette of paint. I'm so happy I took a chance on you. Your friendship is a blessing.
My Sage Poets and my tribe. I love you.
Thank you to all the beautiful souls and living angels who have entered my life and made it into my poetry, including my muses and my loyal fans who encourage and inspire me constantly. I thank the universe for aligning us. Always in perfect timing.
My family. I love you with all that I am.
My mom. Always my most enthusiastic supporter. I love you more than words can say.

If you enjoyed this book, or any of my published works, please consider leaving a review. Thank you!

About the Author

Melody Lee is the author of three celebrated poetry and prose collections: *Moon Gypsy; Vine: Book of Poetry;* and *Season of the Sorceress.* Her poetry has been featured live on Shrimp Shack Ipswich Community Radio, based in the United Kingdom; A Better Media Today, an online magazine; Creative Talents Unleashed, an online collective; Indie Blu(e) Publishing, and Her Red Pen.

Coming April 2021, *Poems for Girls Becoming Women*, an anthology from Workman Publishing.

Signed copies available at
www.etsy.com/your/shops/MelodyLeeEtsyStore
Email: coda.melody@gmail.com
Facebook: www.facebook.com/melodyleepoetry
www.facebook.com/moongypsybymelodylee
Instagram: @melodyleepoetry;
@melodyleequotes; @melodyleebooks
Twitter: www.twitter.com/melodyleepoetry

Made in the USA
Middletown, DE
15 December 2020